LIFE-CHANGING AFFIRMATIONS

A 30-Day Plan *for* Spiritual Transformation

VICKY THOMPSON

Red Wheel
Boston, MA / York Beach, ME

First published in 2005 by
Red Wheel/Weiser, LLC
York Beach, ME
With offices at:
368 Congress Street
Boston, MA 02210
www.redwheelweiser.com
Copyright © 2005 Vicky Thompson

Library of Congress Cataloging-in-Publication Data
Thompson, Vicky.
  Life-changing affirmations : a 30-day plan for spiritual transformation
  Vicky Thompson.
    p. cm.
  ISBN 1-59003-085-0
    1. Spiritual life—Meditations. 2. Affirmations. 3. Devotional
    calendars. I. Title.
  BL624.2.T47 2005
  204′.4—dc22   2005003635

Typeset in Adobe Bembo by Suzanne Albertson
Printed in Canada
TCP

12 11 10 09 08 07 06 05
  8 7 6 5 4 3 2 1

CONTENTS

Introduction

These thirty life-changing affirmations and meditational prayers are powerful spiritual tools for reorienting your emotional compass from down to up. This integrated plan guides you through a thirty-day journey designed to help you achieve a deeper awareness of five keys to spiritual mastery: love, intuition, inner wisdom, forgiveness, and service. Each daily affirmation focuses on a specific spiritual state, giving you the power to direct the flow of vital spiritual qualities into your life.

The daily affirmations are organized into steps, helping you to focus on opening your awareness to mastery of key spiritual qualities. On days 1–5, you use love as a power to fuel change. On days 6–11, you develop an intuitive spiritual practice. Days 12–18 focus on accessing inner wisdom and strength, allowing you to look deeply at your life issues. This understanding helps you to use the tools of forgiveness on days 19–24. Finally, on days 25–30 you use your devotional energy in service of yourself and others.

Most spiritual journeys involve using a daily practice to focus your intentions on aligning with the abundant world of Spirit. The thirty-day plan is designed so that you can cycle through it repeatedly, going deeper each month. You can use the daily affirmations like a calendar, moving through the plan one day at a time. You may choose to focus on a particular step, spending more time working with the affirmations for a specific spiritual quality. You may feel drawn to working on the steps in a different order. Whatever path you choose, follow your heart in creating a daily spiritual practice that reflects your unique journey.

As you use the affirmations during your daily renewal time with Spirit, listen for your own soul balms, which may come to you as new ideas or practices for spiritual healing. You may feel compelled to create your own affirmations or to use the meditational prayers that accompany each daily affirmation. A life-changing spiritual journey is about opening to the power already present within, letting it guide you to a deeper understanding and awareness of the simple richness of life.

How Life-Changing Affirmations Work

Each affirmation strengthens your awareness of your spiritual power, creating life-changing results. Say the daily affirmation out loud, holding the intention to explore this specific spiritual state on this day. As you go through your day, be aware of how this spiritual state affects your interactions with others, your perception of events, and your feeling of spiritual connection with God. Affirm your intention to let this spiritual state flow into your conscious awareness by saying the affirmation throughout the day or by simply affirming, *I am (spiritual state)*. When you encounter a challenge during the day, let the spiritual state help guide your response by saying, *What would (spiritual state) do?*

As you complete each spiritual mastery step, reflect upon your experiences with the spiritual states. Did you feel resistant to or empowered by certain affirmations? When using spiritual states to guide you through difficult situations, did you feel a change in your behavior? Did you notice times when your behavior, thoughts, or feelings were not in alignment with the spiritual state? As you continue to use the affirmations in subsequent months, you will go deeper in your exploration of these spiritual states and develop your ability to allow them to guide you through life.

The affirmations work in concert to create a deeper awareness of your inner spirituality. Knowing that God's *grace* exists within you right now is the first step of a spiritual journey. This seed of grace gives you great *power* to step forward with courage and strength to let go of patterns and behaviors that do not serve you or others well in life. To make lasting changes in your life, you access your power of *creativity* to find new ideas for living life in a deeper, more fulfilling way.

By using your inner power, you tap into your ability to practice *acceptance* of yourself, others, and the deep spiritual world of nature, human beings, and the divine surrounding you. When you recognize the underlying energy propelling the universe, you link with the creative force of *love* to create lasting change.

You use the power of love to create an intuitive spiritual *practice* based on the principles of *discernment*, which provide a road map for releasing what is inessential to love and embracing what is germane to love. Using the intuitive tools of *vision*, *knowing*, *hearing*, and *feeling* leads you back to your heart of inner *wisdom*, deepening your understanding of yourself and others.

Tapping into this great *inspiration* strengthens your *faith* in the often intangible world of God and Spirit, giving you great *hope* that you are ready to face the *truth* of your existence. As you discover your divine purpose in life, you find great *strength* to forge a new path based on the laws of spiritual *abundance*.

When you experience this richness of life, a newfound *vitality* for living fully, deeply, and with great *passion* flows forth, creating a world where you live in *unity* with others. In this place of oneness, you find the true meaning of the spirit of *generosity*: having *compassion* for others, recognizing the commonality of the life experiences and good intentions of all people, and sharing the gift of *forgiveness* with others who have fallen short of their best intentions.

Feeling a new *devotion* to accepting and loving others, you are ready to be of *service* to humanity by becoming a reflection of inner and outer *peace*. By embracing the serenity within, you embody *tranquility*. In this moment, *gratitude* fills your heart with *joy*.

Let the journey begin!

Using Love As the Power for Change

Each spiritual journey begins with a step forward—the moment when you realize that there's more to life than you've been living. Using love as the power for change, you open to the ever-present grace, power, creativity, and acceptance within. Focus on love as you explore the possibility of being more than you are in this moment.

Day 1: *Grace*

When the river flows, grace is here.
When the bird soars, grace is here.
When the sun shines, grace is here.
When I forgive, grace is here.
When I love, grace is here.
When I remember, grace is here.
God's grace smoothes my way.
Grace becomes the road of my journey.
The grace of God becomes me.

Visualize a rainbow of colors streaming down from the heavens, wrapping you in the grace of God as you say the following prayer:

Dear God, I hold your grace within me. I call upon grace to mend hearts I have hurt, to let go of sorrows and regrets, to illuminate my path with truth, and to bless others I have known and will meet upon my journey. Amen.

Day 2: *Power*

The power and strength of God are my own hand.

When I reach out to touch the hand of God, I touch
  my own.

When I look to God for guidance, I look within.

When I hold compassion for others, I hold myself
  in esteem.

I am the power of the heavens.

I am the power of the wind.

I am the power of God.

I flow freely and fully.

See yourself standing on a mountaintop. The sun shines brightly, illuminating you and creating a golden glow around your body. This golden light surges through your body, filling you with the power of God as you say the following prayer:

Dear God, I hold your wisdom, power, and strength. Let your ways be known to me. I accept your power and grace to live a deeper life of communion with you, and my brothers and sisters. Amen.

Day 3: *Creativity*

As God created the universe, the seed of creation was
  planted in me.
I nurture this energy of creation, allowing it to change
  my heart.
I acknowledge behavior that does not serve me well.
I open my seed of creativity, inviting new ways of
  living to flow forth.
In this moment, I create heaven on Earth in me.

See yourself dipping a paintbrush into a can of rich orange paint. As you sweep the brush across the canvas of your life, see it painting over experiences that you want to release. As the old events and behaviors are swept away, see new ways of living take form on the canvas. See yourself living the life God intends for you, as you say the following prayer:

Dear God, I hold your blessed power of creation. Show me how to find new ways of living that reflect the great love you hold for me. Through dreams, friends, and other messengers, illuminate my path through the power of your creative grace. Amen.

Day 4: *Acceptance*

I accept my divine path in life.

I accept the power and presence of Spirit to guide me
on my path.

I accept the inner mastery of others to follow their
own divine plan.

I accept the divinity within all things.

I honor myself, others, nature, and God.

See the heavens open above you. A great angel appears through the clouds, descending slowly to fully embrace you in a loving hug. A feeling of total acceptance fills your being as you say the following prayer:

Dear God, you accept me fully, just as I am. You see the greatness dwelling within me. I accept your divine plan for me. I accept my inner divinity, allowing it to touch all hearts I meet. I accept and allow this inner grace to smooth the road of my journey. Amen.

Day 5: *Love*

I am the love of the world.

I am the light of the world.

When I stand in the light, the darkness fades and my
true heart is revealed.

I choose love and light to guide me.

I choose hope and peace for you, my friend.

Love is the provider, the teacher, the lover, the friend,
the gardener of my soul.

Love is the heart of my soul.

I love you as I love myself.

See a pink light flow down from the heavens and envelop your body. Like a warm, loving embrace, this love melts into your body. You feel like a child, held in the loving arms of God. Love becomes you, and in this safe place, all experiences that were not loving begin to gently flow away from your being. The pink light wraps around these experiences and gently pulls them from your body, returning them to the heavens. Loving pink light continues to flow through you as you say the following prayer:

Dear God, let love become me. Let me remember my heart of love, and let it touch all whom I meet. I am blessed by the love I have always held within. I am love. Amen.

Developing an Intuitive Spiritual Practice

Developing an intuitive spiritual practice requires discernment. Using your intuition, you learn how to listen to your inner voice of wisdom and let go of limiting painful thoughts. This step can be exhilarating as you tap into a new-found awareness of the presence of angels all around you, the messengers between heaven and Earth. Focus on the love of God, letting this strength guide you to a deeper understanding of your spiritual intuition.

Day 6: *Practice*

I am committed to my spiritual growth.

Like a stream rushing after the rain, I open my heart
to the practical graces of God.

I accept the will of my higher spirit-self as my own.

I accept divine guidance for creating my own
spiritual path.

I accept patience for releasing the past and focusing
on the present.

Like nourishing honey overflowing a cup, I let the
life-nectar of God flow abundantly through me.

I am committed to practicing a Spirit-driven life.

Open your arms to the heavens and visualize rain gently falling upon your body, washing away pain and fears, and filling you with the grace of God, as you say the following prayer:

Dear God, I live my life in concert with the divine power, unity, and grace that you always provide. Through your strength, I walk a practical path to my inner heart of wisdom in every moment. I remember my spiritual power and allow it to shine forth through a practice that guides my choices, actions, thoughts, and feelings. Amen.

Day 7: *Discernment*

I see the physical world, but I look deeper.

I hear words spoken, but I listen deeper.

I feel the impact of actions, but I sense deeper.

I know many things about life, but I discern deeper.

I am an observer of life, noticing patterns, choices,
and paths.

I am a participant of life, living in the heart of
the moment.

I am a discerner of life, perceiving the underlying love
empowering all moments.

I look for love, allowing it to guide my way.

Visualize a brilliant white dove flying across the star-filled night sky. The dove looks so clear and bright that sometimes it blends into the stars, making it hard for you to see it. Imagine that the dove is the light of pure love, making it instantly visible to your discerning eyes as you say the following prayer:

Dear God, let your light illuminate my path. I understand the world more clearly through your eyes. I see the heart of love in others and all creations on Earth when I remember that I am the pureness of love. Amen.

Day 8: *Vision*

I see clearly through the haze of doubt and confusion.

I see images of God, visions of heavenly worlds beyond
this earthly world.

In this light, I see the true vision of life.

I am light eternal.

I am love eternal.

I see through the lens of love, opening my inner vision
in all moments.

I see as God sees.

See indigo light stream quickly down from the heavens, surrounding your body like a chrysalis. This powerful light expands and fills the world around you until the entire Earth is one great indigo-colored ball. In this light, you see the divine world coexisting with the earthly world. You see powerful angels guiding and protecting your friends and loved ones. You see energy emanating from all living things, like rays from the sun. You see yourself as a powerful stream of light as you say the following prayer:

Dear God, I see the world as it truly exists through the power and wonder of your grace. I accept my inner vision, my eyes of God. Let me see others as you see me. Let me look deeper, understanding that love is always present in every moment. Amen.

Day 9: *Knowing*

The flame of knowledge lives within me.

In a flash of light, I know all.

In the light of inspiration, I remember my God-given wisdom.

I willingly allow this inner wisdom to light my way.

I access these kernels of insight to guide me in every moment.

I know the truth of my existence.

I am love.

Visualize a wise old teacher sitting on a bench in a beautiful garden. As you sit at the feet of the master, you look up to see your own face staring back at you. You become the master teacher, allowing this eternal wisdom to flow into your conscious awareness as you say the following prayer:

Dear God, I am your light of eternal wisdom. I look to you for guidance, knowing that I am dipping into the well of universal knowledge. Through your power, I allow inner wisdom to flow freely and fully into my mind and heart, forever changing my view of the world and my place in it. Amen.

Day 10: *Hearing*

As I hear the birds singing, the voices of angels
  harmonize joyfully.
As I listen to the wind, the whispers of God speak
  softly.
As I talk with friends, the laughter of Spirit rings truly.
I listen for the voice of God to guide me.
That still, small voice within is my own.

Sense the world of sound around you. Listen to the ever-present sound of nature, the flow of life's traffic outside your window, and the underlying silence of existence. See the source of all sound as the loving light of God, empowering the universe, as you say the following prayer:

Dear God, I hear you clearly. I listen for your wisdom through the words of friends, through the gentle sounds of nature soothing my soul, and through those wondrous moments when I hear your truth speaking through my own voice of wisdom. I listen quietly for this inner wisdom, giving great attention and care to the ever-present voice of truth within. Amen.

Day 11: *Feeling*

Spirit is with me every moment of the day.

When I feel happy, I am embraced by God's love.

When I feel sad, I sense the presence of angels
around me.

When I feel angry, I am aware of Spirit's truth
within me.

When I feel joy, I experience heaven on Earth.

Spirit touches my heart, guiding me through life.

MEDITATIONAL PRAYER

Feel the presence of God in the room. Sense a gentle hand caressing your back, soothing your wounds. Feel a warmth within your belly growing, filling your entire body with love as you say the following prayer:

Dear God, I feel your presence within and around me always. I open my heart to you, letting your light become my own. Amen.

 STEP 3

Accessing Inner Wisdom and Strength

The blessings of a spiritual journey are the fruits of faith: wisdom, inspiration, hope, and abundance. These powerful spiritual states give you strength to face the truth of your life and live as a powerful agent of spiritual change. Life loses its uncertainty when you step forward with confidence on your spiritual path. Focus on opening your heart completely to the wisdom of your inner self.

Day 12: *Wisdom*

I am the light and truth of God.

I am the wisdom of the universe.

I hold this great energy within me now.

Like an ancient book of knowledge, I open my pages
    for all to see.

I let this wisdom flow freely and fully from my being.

I follow my inner wisdom in every moment.

I am the light and truth of God.

In your mind's eye, see yourself sitting at a table in an old castle. The candles burn brightly beside you as you study the book of your existence. In this sacred place, you know what is in the book even before you read its pages. You feel as if you are remembering your favorite play, knowing all of the lines, and the twists and turns in the story. You smile as the wisdom of life energizes your heart and sheds light upon your spiritual path. You feel as if you are embracing eternal truth as you say the following prayer:

Dear God, I hold your wisdom within. I am the brilliant light of your love, illuminating my every choice, action, thought, and feeling. I am wisdom. Amen.

Day 13: *Inspiration*

The heavenly muse of God touches my heart.

I am inspired to live life more deeply and fully in
the light.

Through this spiritual inspiration, I see the juice of life
flowing in every moment.

This rich energy, ripe with possibilities, nourishes my
chosen path.

With great ease and simplicity, I lead a Spirit-driven
life.

See yourself lying on the grass in a flower-filled meadow. Sunlight dapples the ground, and you can smell the heady fragrance of spring blooms. Losing all sense of separation between your body and the earth, you merge with the energy of creation. You are the flowers, you are the grass blades, you are the sunlight. You become the juice of creation, the power of light and growth, as you say the following prayer:

Dear God, I am the flowing river of creativity. I am inspired by your creations. I recognize this creative energy within, allowing it to provide power for my own journey through life. Amen.

Day 14: *Faith*

In faith, God, I remember you.

When I lift my eyes to see your face, God, faith shines
brightly in the darkness.

When I open my heart to your love, God, faith holds
the door for me to step through.

When I walk beside you, God, faith lights my way.

Faith is love without vision.

Faith exists without knowledge or understanding.

Faith simply says, *Yes, because you are, God.*

See yourself walking down a dark hallway. At the end of the corridor, you see a small pinpoint of light. With great purpose, you keep walking toward the light. As you near this illumined point, you realize that you've been following the light streaming through the keyhole of a door. You open the door, stepping into the brilliant sunlight of a heavenly garden. You feel as if you've never left this divine place, as you say the following prayer:

Dear God, my faith in the unseen workings of the divine world is unshakable. I know that you are watching over my every step and that angels are guiding me through each moment of my day. I live with grace, empowered by the faith of love. Amen.

Day 15: *Hope*

Hope enters the world, riding on the wings of peace.
All hope is born of love and peace.
When I hope for peace, I hold great possibilities
    within me.
Like a seed hungering for water, hope waits eternally
    for the flame of God to ignite its power.
I hope for all things, for all things are possible.
I hope for peace, faith, love, and tranquility for all.
Hope is all.

Feeling a tingling sensation in your heart, you remember a moment from childhood when you felt great anticipation for an upcoming event. You remember how a simple outing could fill you with great hope and joy. Let this feeling grow now within your heart, imbuing you with the power of hope as you say the following prayer:

Dear God, this love, this eternal hope, flows within me, enriching my life and the lives of others. I am hope in action, igniting a flame of divine desire in the hearts of all I meet. I let your hope change my view of the world. Amen.

Day 16: *Truth*

In the light, I know truth.

In the light, I seek my inner wisdom.

In the light, I find my hidden heart of love and peace.

In the light, I remember the world of God as my own.

From light to light, I become the light of the world.

I know all through light.

I love all through light.

I honor all through light.

I hold all in the light of truth.

Visualize a mountain stream rushing by your feet. Reflecting the bright sunlight, the water looks like liquid silver. You step into the water, feeling its refreshing energy eddy around your legs. A whirlpool forms around you, pulling all feelings of pain and fear from your body down through your feet. Feeling refreshed and alive, you step from the water as you say the following prayer:

Dear God, I am the light of peace, faith, love, and tranquility. I am your light of light, your beacon of truth. Amen.

Day 17: *Strength*

The light of Spirit is my strength, my all.

Shining boldly and brightly, I illuminate my choices
with great clarity.

Radiating the light of the universe, I touch others with
compassion and love.

Living my life as a divine human vessel, I let my
divinity shine forth.

I am the light of God, a beacon of power showing the
way through heaven and Earth.

This great energy of life is my own.

See yourself as the great sun of the universe. Glowing brightly and providing nourishing rays for life on Earth, you are the strength of every living thing. Your strength is endless and all-encompassing. This power surges effortlessly through you as you say the following prayer:

Dear God, your strength is my own. I am a powerful being of love and peace. I let this strength guide my actions and choices, ensuring that I am a great being of integrity and honor. Amen.

Day 18: *Abundance*

God's grace fills my soul, and I am blessed by the
divine harvest.

God's love holds my hand, and I am embraced by the
divine bounty.

In this world of pain, I sometimes forget my flowing
heart.

In my fear, I leave behind my heavenly seeds.

But in God's abundance, I remember the master
gardener in me.

In God's fields, I find my faith.

In God's streams, I see my love flowing.

In God's creations, I feel my compassion strengthen.

In this world of abundance, I accept the gift of life.

Breathe deeply and slowly, feeling the nourishing breath of life move through you as you say the following prayer:

Dear God, I remember my flowing heart of peace. Through the power you gave to me in the breath of life, I accept your abundance freely. I accept my free will to choose a life of peace. I accept your love to create experiences that let me explore my inner self through this outer world you have made for me. I accept it all, knowing that love is the source of all the wonders of this world. I honor you and my brothers and sisters in this abundant world of love. Amen.

 **STEP 4**

Using the Tools of Forgiveness

The tools of forgiveness remind you of what already exists in great abundance within— vitality and passion to live in unity with others. When you feel whole, you act in generous ways. Your kindhearted actions help you to understand that everyone acts with good intentions, but sometimes people can fall short of doing their best. Forgiveness is the loving culmination of your compassionate desire to live in harmony with others.

Day 19: *Vitality*

I am bursting with delight in the world around me.
Children laughing, birds singing, stars shining bright.
I am the energy of life in all things.
Vitality surges through my body, lightening my load.
I run, hop, and skip through life, never holding to
    the past.
I am the music of the great dance of life.

Take a deep breath and exhale slowly. Take another slow, deep breath, and as you exhale, let out a hearty laugh. As you laugh, see golden sparkles of light dancing around you, like tiny angels of joy, as you say the following prayer:

Dear God, I hold your joy of life and vitality. Life is effortless, filled with wondrous moments of unity with others. I let your energy make this amazing journey possible. Amen.

Day 20: *Passion*

Passion ignites my heart, filling me with the desire to
be one with others.

With great enthusiasm, I see myself as an important
player in life's drama.

My love is needed, my joy is required, my faith is
essential.

I let God's passion stir my soul, creating power for
living, serving, and loving.

See a stream of violet light flowing down from the heavens, embracing you in a dance of passion. Twirling you around, gently tickling your tummy and ruffling your hair, this passion ignites joy within you. Dance with the passion of life as you say the following prayer:

Dear God, I accept the gift of divine passion. Through this loving energy of commitment, I desire to forgive others with compassionate understanding. I embrace life and all of its experiences as you embrace me—with passion. Amen.

Day 21: *Unity*

I am an important part of the unity of the universe.

Like the petal of a flower, I am needed in the structure
of the world.

I share my wholeness with others, feeling in sync with
humanity.

I openly embrace all others along the path of my
journey.

We are one and the same creation of God.

Visualize a jigsaw puzzle of the Earth. With great care, you fit each continent, country, and ocean into its place. As you create the Earth, you remember God's love in creating you and humanity's brothers and sisters. Feel your own uniqueness as well as the unity of humanity, as you say the following prayer:

Dear God, your light and wisdom bless my every moment. In others, I see the light of you, remembering the care and love you feel for me. In myself, I feel the unity and harmony of your existence shining forth and illuminating my path. Amen.

Day 22: *Generosity*

I give to others what God gives to me.

A warm place to rest my head, guidance to light my
way, and friends to share life.

I let this spirit of generosity move through me.

I fill my life with loving-kindness, serving myself and
others with gratitude.

Breathe deeply, feeling your belly expand with the bounty
of the breath of God. Visualize yourself standing on a grassy
knoll, surrounded by a sea of people. A pink light streams
down from the heavens, completely filling your body. This
intense energy of love cannot be contained in your small
body. It flows forth like the rays of the sun, warming all
souls around you. Feel the spirit of generosity as you say the
following prayer:

*Dear God, I lovingly accept your kindness, and in turn,
I give it to others without conditions. Generosity is like
rain, created from what already exists—the moisture in
the earth and sky. Your seeds of love, compassion, forgiveness, and understanding already exist within me.
From these divine elements of life, I create generosity to
bless myself and all those I know. Amen.*

Day 23: *Compassion*

When God created the world, my friend, it was made
   for you and me.
When God created you, the same love was used to
   make me.
When God created love, Spirit asked me to hold
   compassion for you.
God's loving compassion, I hold it for you.
Through lightness and dark, through joy and hurt,
   my compassionate love, I hold it for you.

See yourself as a small child, sitting on the lap of God as you say the following prayer:

Dear God, I hold your power and strength in this moment to love all who have hurt me. You love me no matter what I do. I extend that love to those who have hurt me. I recognize the wholeness dwelling within these friends. In compassion and love, I hold high the potential of my friends, knowing that they are capable of more than they are demonstrating in this moment. I recognize that I have not shown my true greatness in all situations. Through your love for me, God, I extend this loving compassion to my friends and myself. Amen.

Day 24: *Forgiveness*

Dear heart of love, I let go of this pain.

Dear soul of freedom, I break free from these chains of anger and disappointment.

God knows that sometimes I forget my true heart of love.

God reminds me through divine forgiveness to remember my love.

God lets go of what came before, gracing my path with divine love for what will be.

Dear friend of love, I let go of the pain and forgive what came before.

Through the grace of God, we remember our love and choose what will be.

Visualize friends who have hurt you as standing beside you. A heavenly white light streams down to embrace you all, gently pulling away and releasing all pain. The light ripples, forming a shimmering bubble around you and your friends as you say the following prayer:

Dear God, I hold only love in my heart for my friends. I forgive them for the pain they have caused. I forgive myself for the pain I have caused. I accept the healing light of love, compassion, and acceptance. I hold only the highest and best in my heart for us all. Amen.

Now let go of this experience, knowing that you all hold God's love to move forward without pain or regret. See the bubble gently float to the heavens. Embraced in the loving arms of God, the bubble dissolves into brilliant white light, freeing you all from the past.

 STEP 5

Serving the Self and Others

Inner peace gives rise to a feeling of devotion to humanity, encouraging you to serve others. In serving the self and others, you enter a space of inner tranquility, a calm sanctuary that inspires your outer actions of unity. As you recognize humanity's brothers and sisters as your own, you feel gratitude for the opportunity to assist others on their journey. Joy eternal, rich with happiness and peace, becomes you.

Day 25: *Devotion*

Heaven above, earth below, humanity in between,
  I honor all of God's creations.
Blessed flowers, flowing rivers, mountains high,
  nature's beauty is God's mirror of our beauty
  within.
Water, earth, fire, and air,
  I honor all of God's creations.
I honor God and the heavens above me.
I honor God and the earth below me.
I honor God and the humanity in me.

Visualize yourself standing on a mountaintop. Below you lies the earth and above you looms the sky. See a star forming in your heart, growing from the center of your being until it touches the earth and the sky. Feeling a great sense of love and centeredness, say the following prayer:

Dear God, I feel your devotion when a kind word is spoken. I know your presence is near when the wind ruffles my hair. I feel peace when you lift my spirits. This divine devotion lives through me when I honor this world you created for me. Amen.

Day 26: *Service*

My brothers and sisters, I know you through God.

As God shines through my heart, I shine the light
for you.

As God teaches me about love, I share my lessons
with you.

As God holds me lovingly, I embrace you.

As God whispers in my ear, I laugh with you.

As God uses my able hands, I reach out to you.

Let God work through me.

Let God touch the world through me.

Let God live through me.

Visualize a pink light flowing from the heavens, wrapping you in a gentle embrace. The light ignites the flame of love in your heart, filling you with a great desire to serve yourself and others. The first recipient of this loving service is you. Hold your hands in open acceptance as you say the following prayer:

Dear God, let your will for me be known. Use me as your creation. When a kind word needs to be spoken, use my voice. When a load needs to be lifted, use my back. When a hug needs to be given, use my arms. When a journey needs to be taken, use my feet. When a message needs to be delivered, use my mind. When a friend needs to be loved, use my heart. In all things, in all ways, use me, God, as your instrument of love, faith, peace, and tranquility. Amen.

Day 27: *Peace*

In my hidden heart, I know this feeling.

Deep inside, the river flows with the peace of
the world.

This world, this place of love unbridled, is where you
and I meet.

Alone, but together, silent, but joyful, we share this
deep peace as one.

Peace dwells within me, always waiting patiently,
knowing that I will return to its embrace.

In my heart, I know this place.

In my heart, I am peace.

See yourself walking through a sea of people. As you are bumped and jostled in the crowd, visualize the hand of God reaching down to hold yours as you walk along. You reach out to hold hands with the people next to you, and they in turn reach out to touch others. You feel great peace among humanity as you say the following prayer:

Dear God, let your peace guide me through life. When I feel angry, remind me of my inner compassion. When I feel lonely, remind me of the presence of divine guardians. When I feel afraid, remind me of my inner strength. Remind me of my inner peace, always present, always greater than the obstacles outside of me. Amen.

Day 28: *Tranquility*

In the stillness, I hear my heart beating.
In a shaft of sunlight, I see the gentle fluttering of a
butterfly.
My heart matches the beat of its small wings.
As the butterfly soars into the air,
so do I remember this freedom.
A world without walls, simple moments of life.
I close my eyes and I am there.
In the silence, tranquility rises from within.

See yourself gently awakened by the sunlight of a new day. As you part the curtains, you see divine light surrounding your everyday landscape. A great calmness and a sense of assuredness infuse your body as you say the following prayer:

Dear God, I am your peace of the world. I embody this tranquility within. I enter this retreat to remember my strength in living a life driven by the power and presence of Spirit. I am one with Spirit in all things and all ways. Amen.

Day 29: *Gratitude*

For the heavens that light my way, I thank you.
For the Earth that supports all life, I thank you.
For days and nights filled with love, I thank you.
For experiences that remind me of grace, I thank you.
In all ways, in all things, I thank you.

See all of the wonders of life: family and friends, the beauty of nature, inspiring moments, and the presence of God in all things. Reflect upon all of the simple things that make your life so rich, as you say the following prayer:

Dear God, thank you in all ways for all blessings. Amen.

Day 30: *Joy*

_____

My heart is bursting with joy in this moment.

When I feel the glory of God beside me, I feel blessed.

When I see the wonder of God's creations, I feel loved.

When I hear the sound of God's whisper in my ear, I
slow down.

When I know how close I am to God, I stop the
world.

In this place of silence, I listen and hear my heartbeat.

In each beat, I sense the tenderness that went into
creating me.

In that delicate fabric of life, I feel honored to live
upon the Earth.

Breathe deeply, inhaling the joy of God. As you exhale, see golden sparkles of joy surrounding you. As these sparkles of heavenly delight dance around you, feel your heart swelling with uncontainable joy as you say the following prayer:

Dear God, I see the same cloth of your creation in all my brothers and sisters. I see the same love, patience, and kindness dwelling within all humanity. I now know that we are all one and the same creation of God. I lay down my judgments and embrace my brothers and sisters in love. I let the same love you created in me touch the same love in all others. In love, in peace, we embrace as one. Joy eternal becomes me, joy present becomes me. Amen.

Counting Your Spiritual Blessings

As you practice the affirmations and meditational prayers, you may glimpse a world of light, love, and wisdom beyond your own. Each person's spiritual journey is unique, filled with wondrous moments of divine revelation and healing. Life expands, evolving from merely passing time on Earth to fully living life in heaven on Earth.

As you open your heart to Spirit, you invite the guiding hand of God to lead you to experiences in fulfillment of your divine path. When you listen with discernment to your inner wisdom, you learn how to accept new thoughts and actions that better serve yourself and humanity.

These blessings of Spirit enrich your life. Accept these kernels of divine wisdom for what they are: gifts from God to help you to remember your inner power and love. When change is painful, remember God's love for you. When you wish to know God's plan for you, use your spiritual intuition. When all seems lost, find your inner strength through divine inspiration. When you and others fall short of doing your best, forgive freely and often. When you feel thankful for God's abundant ways, devote yourself in service to the self and others.

Always count your spiritual blessings for they are always within you.

ABOUT THE AUTHOR

Vicky Thompson applies spiritual wisdom to the practical aspects of everyday living to make sense of life's journey. Using the power of affirmations and meditations has enabled her to heal many of her own life issues, including the pain of childhood abuse. A popular workshop leader and frequent speaker at spiritual expos nationwide, Thompson is also the author of *The Jesus Path: 7 Steps to a Cosmic Awakening* and the creator of the meditation CD *Journey to Spiritual Awakening*. For more spiritual tools, visit her website at *www.journeywithspirit.com*.

TO OUR READERS

Red Wheel, an imprint of Red Wheel/Weiser, publishes books on topics ranging from spunky self-help, spirituality, personal growth, and relationships to women's issues and social issues. Our mission is to publish quality books that will make a difference in people's lives—how we feel about ourselves and how we relate to one another and to the world at large. We value integrity, compassion, and receptivity, both in the books we publish and in the way we do business.

Our readers are our most important resource, and we value your input, suggestions, and ideas about what you would like to see published. Please feel free to contact us, to request our latest book catalog, or to be added to our mailing list.

Red Wheel/Weiser, LLC
P.O. Box 612
York Beach, ME 03910-0612
www.redwheelweiser.com